The Ultimate Small Business Guide

*Discover The 7 Biggest Mistakes
Small Business Owners Make…
And How To Avoid Them Like The Plague*

Efrain Aguilar

Copyright © 2017 Efrain Aguilar. www.luminarmarketing.com

And done very nicely too ☺

All rights reserved.

ISBN-13: 978-1548594732
ISBN-10: 1548594733

DEDICATION

To my loving beautiful wife…my princess bride who supports me in all I do, in my failures and successes. And to my loving four children who are always cheering me on.

ACKNOWLEDGEMTNS

First, thanks to my wonderful and beautiful wife for editing my manuscript many times over and over. This is truly our book, not just my book but ours indeed.

Second, to Valerie Turner who was a tremendous help in editing and correcting all my misspelled words and terrible grammar…Thanks Valerie! You made this book sound and feel much smoother and easier to understand.

CONTENTS

1	NOT HAVING A BUSINESS GPS	13
2	NOT HAVING A USP	20
3	NOT IDENTIFYING YOUR TARGET MARKET… *YOUR NICHE*	26
4	NOT HAVING A LEAD GENERATION SYSTEM	33
5	NOT HAVING A SYSTEMATIC REFERRAL GENERATING SYSTEM	37
6	NOT SEGMENTING YOUR LIST OF CUSTOMERS, CLIENTS, OR PATIENTS	44
7	NOT BEING A MASTER OF TIME MANAGEMENT	46
8	FINAL THOUGHTS	48
9	CONCLUSSION	50
10	WORLD'S GREATEST RESOURCES	51

DISCLAIMER AND TERMS OF USE AGREEMENT
The author and publisher of this book and the associated materials have used their best efforts in preparing this material. The author and publisher make no representations or warranties with respect to the accuracy, applicability, fitness, or completeness of the contents of this material. They disclaim any warranties expressed or implied, merchantability, or fitness for any particular purpose. The author and publisher shall in no event be held liable for any loss or other damages, including but not limited to special, incidental, consequential, or other damages. If you have any doubts about anything, the advice of a competent professional should be sought. This material contains elements protected under International and Federal Copyright laws and treaties. Any unauthorized reprint or use of this material is prohibited

The author and publisher disclaim any warranties (express or implied), merchantability, or fitness for any particular purpose. The author and publisher shall in no event be held liable to any party for any direct, indirect, punitive, special, incidental or other consequential damages arising directly or indirectly from any use of this material, which is provided "as is", and without warranties. As always, the advice of a competent legal, tax, accounting or other professional should be sought. The author and publisher do not warrant the performance, effectiveness or applicability of any sites listed or linked to in this Program. This Program is © copyrighted by Efrain Aguilar. No part of this may be copied, or changed in any format, sold, or used in any way other than what is outlined within this Program under any circumstances.

EVERY EFFORT HAS BEEN MADE TO ACCURATELY REPRESENT THIS PRODUCT AND IT'S POTENTIAL. EVEN THOUGH THIS INDUSTRY IS ONE OF THE FEW WHERE ONE CAN WRITE THEIR OWN CHECK IN TERMS OF EARNINGS, THERE IS NO GUARANTEE THAT YOU WILL EARN ANY MONEY USING THE TECHNIQUES AND IDEAS IN THESE MATERIALS. EXAMPLES IN THESE MATERIALS ARE NOT TO BE INTERPRETED AS A PROMISE OR GUARANTEE OF EARNINGS.

EARNING POTENTIAL IS ENTIRELY DEPENDENT ON THE PERSON USING OUR PRODUCT, IDEAS AND TECHNIQUES. WE DO NOT PURPORT THIS AS A "GET RICH SCHEME." ANY CLAIMS MADE OF ACTUAL EARNINGS OR EXAMPLES OF ACTUAL RESULTS CAN BE VERIFIED UPON REQUEST. YOUR LEVEL OF SUCCESS IN ATTAINING THE RESULTS CLAIMED IN OUR MATERIALS DEPENDS ON THE TIME YOU DEVOTE TO THE PROGRAM, IDEAS AND TECHNIQUES MENTIONED, YOUR FINANCES, KNOWLEDGE AND VARIOUS SKILLS. SINCE THESE FACTORS DIFFER ACCORDING TO INDIVIDUALS, WE CANNOT GUARANTEE YOUR SUCCESS OR INCOME LEVEL. NOR ARE WE RESPONSIBLE FOR ANY OF YOUR ACTIONS.

MATERIALS IN OUR PRODUCT AND OURWEBSITE MAY CONTAIN INFORMATION THAT INCLUDES OR IS BASED UPON FORWARD-LOOKING STATEMENTSWITHIN THE MEANING OF THE SECURITIES LITIGATION REFORMACT OF 1995. FORWARD-LOOKING STATEMENTS GIVE OUR EXPECTATIONS OR FORECASTS OF FUTURE EVENTS. YOU CAN IDENTIFY THESE STATEMENTS BY THE FACT THAT THEY DO NOT RELATE STRICTLY TO HISTORICAL OR CURRENT FACTS. THEY USEWORDS SUCH AS "ANTICIPATE," "ESTIMATE," "EXPECT," "PROJECT," "INTEND," "PLAN," "BELIEVE," AND OTHER WORDS AND TERMS OF SIMILAR MEANING IN CONNECTIONWITH A DESCRIPTION OF POTENTIAL EARNINGS OR FINANCIAL PERFORMANCE.

ANY AND ALL FORWARD LOOKING STATEMENTS HERE OR ON ANY OF OUR SALES MATERIAL ARE INTENDED TO EXPRESS OUR OPINION OF EARNINGS POTENTIAL. MANY FACTORS WILL BE IMPORTANT IN DETERMINING YOUR ACTUAL RESULTS AND NO GUARANTEES ARE MADE THAT YOU WILL ACHIEVE RESULTS SIMILAR TO OURS OR ANYBODY ELSE'S, IN FACT NO GUARANTEES ARE MADE THAT YOU WILL ACHIEVE ANY RESULTS FROM OUR IDEAS AND TECHNIQUES IN OUR MATERIAL.

INTRODUCTION

The Essentials of Starting a Small Business

Over the years, I've seen friends and family start their small business, either online or traditional, only to find themselves frustrated, disappointed, dismayed, and discouraged. They all faced similar problems when starting a small business, either online or traditional brick and mortar. In this book, you will discover the *7 Biggest Mistakes Small Business Owners Make…And How To* **Avoid** *Them Like The Plague.*

According to the SBA, as of 2010, there were approximate 28.8 million small businesses in the Unites States. And of these 28.8 million, over 21 million are self-employed solopreneurs and home-based businesses. The survival rate, in this tough economy, after one year is approximately 75%. After five years, its 48% survival rate. Astonishing is in it! But we shouldn't be surprise with our volatile and multi-challenge economy.

Most small business owners that start a business think that if they open doors and are good at what they do, customers will flock to their stores or websites. No longer true in our current business state. There are millions of small-business owners in the service industries, who are experts at what they do, yet still struggle financially. That's because they are making the same mistake. They are marketing their technical expertise instead of marketing the **BENEFITS** their product or service brings to their customers, clients, or patients.

I wrote this small book so you as a small business owner can **AVOID** the **7 Biggest Mistakes** small business owner make. These are easy to follow steps that you can immediately implement in your small business, regardless of the industry you are in, product or service you sell. So let's get started so you can be a successful small business owner and live the life you have always wanted.

Best of luck in your business endeavor and have the greatest success in your small business.

Efrain Aguilar, MBA

Dear Small Business Owner and Solopreneur

If you are a small business owner or solopreneur and you have said to yourself, *"If I could just Get All The Customers, Clients or Patients I need or want to stay in Business and Live The Life I've always wanted and Be With My Family and Friends"* then this might be the most important book you read all year. Here's why…

Have You ever said any of these things?

- *I am not getting enough customers, clients or patients every month to pay the bills!*

- *I am frustrated with advertising that doesn't work*

- *I am tired of Revenue roller coaster, income going up and down as my flow of new customers, clients or patients changes sporadically…every month*

- *I am Tired of price shoppers that are constantly **nickel-ing** and **dime-ing** me on price*

- *Customers, clients or patients who just don't get it*

- *I **Want** to save time so I can talk only to customers, clients, or patients who are ready to do business with me.*

- *I wish I could double or triple my income in the next six to twelve months so I can live the life I want!*

How Would You Define *Success* As A *Small Business* Owner?

"You have a steady stream of clients who automatically seek out your valuable product or services without you having to do any cold prospecting, chasing, bribing, or begging customers to do business with you. You are viewed with respect by customers, clients, or patients who value your advice. You are able to easily provide them superior service and results which lead them to refer you to others and give you their repeat business. You work a normal work week (or less), take plenty of time off to pursue outside interests, and make a rewarding income to enjoy with friends and family."

Can you describe your small business in this way?

FACT:

Most small business owners **EITHER**:

- Make a **lot of money** and have **no life** outside their small business to enjoy it, OR
- **Have a life** outside their business but **don't make enough money**, OR
- **Kill themselves with grueling 75+ hour week AND barely make enough money to survive…** *to pay the bills!*

Which Of These *Business Characters* Are You?

Imagine You Could Wave a Magic Wand…

Imagine you could wave a magic wand and know that every month you had all the customers or clients you want or need so you can live the life you've always wanted with family and friends.

And imagine this *Magic Wand* could take you to a hidden secret land where your ideal prospects live in abundance…*but none of your competitors know about or can ever visit this hidden land.* You are the only one allowed because of your unique special message to them.

This is what this book is all about. I will help you find that hidden secret land where all your ideal customers, clients, or patients live…you can have all the customers you want or need…at your will.

The experience you will create for your prospects will be so uniquely different than any of your competitors…you'll be the only expert your prospects will seek out…every time!

Just Imagine That!

But let me warn you...this is **NOT** a <u>Get-Rich-Quick Scheme</u>. This requires time, energy, and investment in your marketing. There are no short cuts to profitable marketing. You must be *consistent*, *persistent*, and *resistant* to make marketing work for your business.

This will be a new *Paradigm* shift in your business that will revolutionize the way you think about your small business and how you can approach it in a totally different way…much differently than your competitors. *More about this later.*

Finally, if you already have a list of prospects, I will show you how to find *riches* within your *niches*…segmenting and dissecting your customers', clients' or patients' needs or wants so you can sell more to them and more consistently. Again, this is not quick and easy but requires time, dedication, and energy. *So let's saddle up and hit the road!*

Why Should You Listen To Me?

"I started my marketing consulting business to help small business owners and solopreneurs stay in business by helping them attract more of their ideal customers, clients, or patients every month.

But as a small business owner like yourself, I struggled in the beginning and wondered if I could continue. I was only getting about zero or one clients per month, I was deep in debt, struggling to pay my mortgage, I was thinking about having to get a regular job *(a real job as my friends would say)*.

I then discovered unique and stealth-marketing strategies to attract all the clients I wanted…I understand your struggles and frustrations. I want to show you how you could do the same in your business.

These marketing strategies will work in any industry or business. I've done all the research and hard work for you. These are easy to implement marketing strategies, swipe and deploy campaigns so you can see clients come to you…No more begging, bribing, or chasing them to do business with you…**never again**!"

Before we jump into our first chapter, let me show you a new way of doing business. Regardless of what industry you are in or what type of product or service you sell. This new way of thinking will work in any industry. Have an open mind so you can implement this into your business…you will see the positive changes within the next six to twelve months.

> **WARNING**: the plain truth is that this business model is not for every small business owner. This is **NOT** for everyone.

Take a look at the table below. Your particular type of business can use and implement this model. You might have to tweak it a little bit…but the model and the process is still the same.

If you're looking for quick incremental improvements in your sales, than this might not be for you. This requires consistency and commitment.

This model will radically transform your ordinary business into a unique selling business machine…consistently. Just implement these marketing tactics and strategies into your business and the results will follow!

Here's a new way of thinking…

X Chasing prospects who really don't want to do business with you	✓ Compel prospects to CALL YOU using emotional Direct Response Marketing
X Working with customers, clients or patients you don't like because you "**Have**" to.	✓ Use technology to AUTOMATICALLY sift, sort, and screen your leads to find the most qualified ready-to-act prospects
X Slave to every poorly qualified prospect who doesn't value you or your time	✓ Work ONLY with prospects you WANT to work with…*those who will do things your way and NOT fight you every minute.*
X Wasting tons of money on advertising that doesn't work. Zilch!	✓ Present compelling benefits to these prospects, giving them specific and tangible reasons to want to work with you WITHOUT ANY selling, chasing, or bribing.
X Frustrated with customers, clients or patients that are constantly nickel-ing and dime-ing you on price.	✓ Work ONLY with those who value your products or services and who will work with you under those terms… DISCARD THE REST
X Tired revenue roller coaster, income going up and down as your flow of new customers changes sporadically	✓ Consistently attract more of your best customers, clients, or patients at will and dominate your target market
X Sick and tired of being sick and tired	✓ LOVE what you're doing. Have fun HELPING qualified and sincere customers, clients or patients who are loyal to you.
X **Sick of your business**	✓ Be FREE to enjoy a rewarding personal life AND run a profitable business… *AT THE SAME TIME*

NOT HAVING A BUSINESS GPS

A Business GPS

A GPS is used to get you from where you are now to where you want to get in the fastest or shortest distance without getting lost. So, what is your *Business GPS?* It is your **Business Plan** and **Marketing Plan**. A business plan is the make-it or break-it business thermometer.

A business plan will help you prepare and anticipate changes in your business market. You want to know how much cash you will need to start up, your monthly expenses, and the cash on hand you need to pay the bills to stay in business. You may have revenues but not fast enough to pay the current bills.

These are import items you need to know before starting a business. For example, your business plan, in a nutshell will include the following:

If you are starting a Shoe Company

1. A Goal: A broad primary outcome
   - We want to be the best outdoor shoe company on planet earth within the next three years.

2. A Strategy: The approach you take to achieve your goal
   - Persuade outdoor enthusiasts that our shoes are the best in the market

3. An Objective: The measurable steps you take to achieve a strategy
   - Capture 70 percent or more of the worldwide outdoor market

4. A Tactic: The tools you will use in pursuing the objective associated with the strategy

- Using messages via Social Media or Direct Response marketing and using partner brand awareness, celebrities or professionals using our shoes.

Where are You Going?
Your business plan will help you determine your vision, goals, strategies, objectives, and tactics. Your business plan in a sense is your battleground strategy. Your business plan helps you determine where you want to be in one year, three years, five years, and seven years. It is vitally important to know where you want to go to make the necessary plans and adjustments along the way.

Without a business plan, you will be lost, discouraged at times, wasteful, and unproductive. A business plan also helps you stay focused on activities that bring you results and income.

> You must also plan to spend time **ON** your business and not too much **IN** your business, more about that later.

How Will You Get There?

Your business plan also determines the tools that you will use to get where you want to go. What resources will you use? How much cash will you spend on marketing and advertising? How much do you have to sell to break even and stay in business?

How much do you need to sell to reach your income goals per month, quarter, and year? You must answer these questions before you start your business. I've included an outline of a one-page business plan in the Bonus section. Remember, don't Fire and then Aim, but **Aim** first then **Fire**.

Your Marketing Plan…Another Key Ingredient to Your Business Success
Your marketing plan is your plan for how to get prospects knocking on your door or visiting your website.
- How are you going to attract them
- How are you going to convey your message to them

- What media will you use to attract them
- How often are you going to market to them

These are all key questions you need to ask yourself. Without customers, clients, or patients, you don't have a business at all. Plain and simple vanilla!

But, to simplify things, your marketing plan can boil down to Three Key Ingredients.

1. *Market*
2. *Message*
3. *Media*

This is your marketing plan in a simple nutshell. Let's cover each one of these briefly.

Your Market
First, you must understand and know your customers, clients, or patients to make easy sales.

To develop a successful marketing plan, you need to know the following four Key Points.

1. Who are your customers, clients, or patients
2. What is it that they want
3. What motivates them to want to buy
4. How will you motivate them to buy from you instead of your competition

Ask yourself these primary questions to fully understand your market

- How does my potential customer, client, or patient normally buy similar products or service
    - Online
    - Brick and mortar
    - Door-to-door
    - Mail orders
    - Mobile devices

- Who is the primary buyer and decision maker in the purchasing process
    - Husband
    - Wife
    - CEO
    - Leader
    - Manager
    - Office manager

- What kinds of habits do my customers, clients, or patients have? Where do they get their information before purchasing my product or service?
    - TV
    - Newspaper
    - Magazines
    - Online
    - Social Media

- What are my target customer's, client's, or patient's primary motivations for purchasing my product or service
    - Avoid pain
    - Get healthy
    - Look fabulous
    - Be popular and beat the Jones's

One big mistake that business owners make when marketing to their target market is thinking as if they are their own customer. Plain and simple, don't confuse *"Wants"* with *"Needs."*

Prospects don't buy what they really need, but they'll always, or most of the time, buy what they want. For example, people who go to the grocery store to purchase a gallon of milk, a dozen eggs, and a loaf of bread usually come out with other items like cookies, coke, beer, cake, and pizza. People will buy what they want, even if they don't have the money to buy those things. They will make a way to do it!

These principles also apply to big corporations when they are selling their products or services.

Choose a Niche Within Your Target Market

Most business owners are inclined to market to everyone. But when you market to everyone, **you are marketing to no one**.

You must pick a niche to target, and then become the expert at that niche. People love to work with specialists. Be a specialist in your niche. Start by picking one niche from your target market. Dominate that specific niche in your market; then move on to another niche within your target market. The possibilities are endless.

Here are some examples of niches within a target market:
- Insurance agent
    - *For Professional athlete insurance*
    - *Small business insurance*
    - *Malpractice insurance for dentist*
- C.P.A
    - *For small business owners only*
    - *Childcare business*
    - *Realtors*
- Contractor
    - *Specializes in decks only*
    - *Room additions only*
    - *Kitchens only*

To close this up, let me give you my **Simple 7 Step Marketing Plan**

Step 1 - Understand Your Market and Competition
Step 2 - Understand Your Customer, Clients or Patients
Step 3 - Pick a Niche *(narrow your market)*
Step 4 - Develop Your Marketing Message specific to your niche
Step 5 - Determine Your Marketing Medium(s) *(the best possible one)*
Step 6 - Set Sales and Marketing Goals
Step 7 - Develop Your Marketing Budget
Bonus – Monitor and Measure Results

Your Message
Your marketing message is critical and must be written to your specific target market or niche.

You should develop two different marketing messages, actually you will develop several, but two important ones are:
1. Your elevator pitch to quickly tell people what you do and how you can help them
2. Your second message is written directly to your niche...

Your Message To Market Match
If you have several niches, your marketing material will be written differently for each niche. It's the best and fastest way to attract your ideal customer, client, or patient.

You will probably use your second marketing message in most of your marketing materials and promotions. So how do you create your marketing message. Well, it really depends on your industry and your target market. But, here are some simple steps when creating your marketing message.

Your message must be compelling and persuasive:

- It should have your target prospect's problem or pain
- Convince your prospects that their problem is a major pain and needs to be solved now
- Explain why you're the only solution in solving your prospect's problem/pain
- Explain the benefits your prospects will receive from using your solution: product or services
- Use testimonial to gain trust
- Explain your unconditional guarantee

Your Media
Next is your marketing media or mediums. This is how you will communicate with your prospects and past clients on a regular basis. This is how you will deliver your marketing message.

It's very important that you choose the right media to deliver your marketing message. Choose the one that will give you the highest return on your marketing investment, **ROI**.
Choose a marketing media that will deliver your message to the most

prospects within your niche at the lowest possible price, but not all the time.

Sometimes the cheapest may give you very lousy results. So don't always choose the cheapest. *Do your homework*.

Use the following tools to get your message across to your niche. These are just a few. Find different ways to deliver your message

- Social Media
- Online
- Postcards…*Direct Response Marketing*
- Newspaper ads
- Flyers
- Newsletter
- Emails
- Magazine ads

To get it Spot On:

You must match your message to your specific target market or niche using the right medium to bang the greatest results! In simpler words…*who is your message supposed to resonate with*.

So, do your homework to determine which media is right for your message to attract your best prospects who are ready and willing to do business with you.

Your Message Must Convey The Following:
- Identify the **PROBLEM** your prospects have
- **AGITATE** the problem your prospects have
- Show them how you can **SOLVE** their problem
- **TELL** exactly what you want them to do

NOT HAVING A USP

How can you blow the competition away and make everyone else irrelevant? If you don't differentiate yourself from everyone else, you're just another business on the block…a commodity.

Without a **USP**, you are like all your competitors. **BORING!**

USP stands for *Unique Selling Proposition*. This is what makes you stand out from all others in the business. You set yourself apart with a USP.

Let me give you some examples of well known **USP**'s:

- *"Fresh, hot pizza delivered in 30 minutes or less, guaranteed."* Dominos Pizza. (target to students)
- *"When it absolutely, positively has to be there overnight."* Fedex.
- *"Leaves your breath smelling minty fresh."* Scope.

Your **USP** must always convey a benefit that your clients, customers, or patients can identify with. Don't talk about your features such as, "we've been in business for 30 years, or combined experience of 200 years, blah, blah, blah." Baloney, phooey. I *cringe* when I see businesses advertise they have 220 years of combined experience.

Your prospects don't care about your features. They care about what benefits them. How can you solve their problem.

> Your prospects **don't care** about your features. They care about what **benefits them**. *How can you solve their problem.*

Your *USP* must be very specific, to the point, and targeted to your specific audience. Make your USP to the point and short if possible.

Let's look at Dominos Pizza's *USP*. First, they don't claim that their

pizza tastes better than any other pizza on planet earth. They are only claiming that it will get there fast and hot!
There USP is also very specific...will get there in 30 minutes, guaranteed.

Your *USP* must also be short, no more than two sentence at the most. Too long of a *USP* and you can lose your prospect's thoughts.

The point is to make your suspects and prospects remember your *USP* so the next time they are in need of someone to solve their problem, they will immediately think of you.

Ok. So here are your **3 Steps** to Creating a *Unique Selling Proposition*. This will take some time to develop your unique selling proposition. Be patient and brain storm this.

1. Go to Office Depot, Staples, or Office Max and purchase 3x5 index cards

One side of the card you will write a feature of your business and on the other side, you will write down a benefit of your product or service. For example, a seat belt is a feature; the material it's made of is a feature. The benefit is that it will save your life or save lives.

- A bakery: a cake that's made of all natural ingredients is a feature and the benefit is that parents will be happy their children will be eating healthy and still having a good time!

- A florist: long stem roses are a feature and the benefit is that the recipient will be able to enjoy them longer at home or the office.

- An automaker: a 100-miles-per-gallon vehicle is the feature and the benefit is that car owners will be able to spend more money on their vacation with family and friends.

These are just a few examples for you to start writing some of your own features and benefits for your specific business.

2. The next step is to find out what your competition is saying

Go through your yellow pages, see what businesses similar to yours are saying, and make note of that. Again, this takes time, but once you do this, it will dramatically increase your income.

Make a list of features and benefits that your competition is claiming. Most likely, your competition is just screaming their features and saying nothing about their benefits whatsoever.

So, here is the million-dollar question,

"So why should a client contact you as opposed to any other business like yours if everyone else is saying the same thing?"

You might be inclined to say, "I am better," but how does your prospect know that? Everyone else is saying the same thing. This is known as marketing incest…*everyone is copying each other*.

No difference from one business to the next!

There are no advantages from your business to the guys down the street. With a clear, specific, to-the-point USP, your prospects will know you can solve their problem, and they will be calling you…instead of you chasing them.

You need to stand out from all the rest of the gold fish in the fish bowl. You need to be perceived as being different and unique.

A quick note here: you may be offering the same features and service as your competition. And that is perfectly fine. However, frame your features in a way so you're perceived as being different from your competitors. Package your product or service differently.

Or find a way you can be different from your competitors. Your prospects will immediately see you as different from all the rest and will immediately call you and not your competitors.

So, now that you've researched your competition and prepared your

3x5 cards, you can now start writing some USP's. Again, this may take a few days to finally come up with one unique *USP* that stands out.

3. The final step in creating a USP

Your USP must answer this one question and only this question:

> **"Why should I hire you, as opposed to anyone else…**
> *(whatever business you're in)***."**

And now, saying you are the best or you have 220 years of combined experience does not cut it.

Not in this economy.

<u>**How To Use Your USP**</u>

Once you've create your USP, you will use it in every marketing material you create and also use it on your business card.

Use it on your voice mail, when you answer the phone at your office, your mail pieces, brochures, and advertising. Use it everywhere you can.

When you say your USP, prospects will ask, "How do you do that," or "Tell me more about that." This is the chief cornerstone of all the marketing materials you design.

The difference between successful and unsuccessful small business owners is that successful business owners do all the things that unsuccessful people don't like or don't want to do.

Don't get me wrong, successful business owners don't like to do them either, but they do them anyway. That's what makes them successful small business owners.

How About You My Friend. What type of business character are you?

Are you willing to take these steps to make your business dreams come true about your business? I believe the answer is yes. I strongly believe that it's true or you wouldn't have invested in this book.

Do you see how easy this is to do! This is an incredible opportunity for you to create a competitive advantage! Especially if you're in an industry known for crappy service or thought of as a commodity…

Same ole, same ole…pretty much every industry.

<u>Rock bottom line</u>: any business in any industry, in any economy can find a path to success by delivering outstanding service that surprises and delights its customers, clients, or patients.

And I'll get on the phone with you and prove it to you!

Here's how…

If you try out my *Ultimate Client Attraction System in a Box*, I'll give you a 20-minute No Brainer Session by phone. You could be just 20 minutes away from an extraordinary breakthrough.

You have nothing to lose but everything to gain!

http://www.luminarmarketing.com/client-attraction

BONUS

7 Things You Must <u>NEVER</u> Do In Your USP Marketing

- Focus on yourself rather than the customer, client, or patient
- Make a vague and unsubstantiated claim or statement
- Believe that if "They Know Who I am They Will Call Me And Use My Product/Service" Nope! Not in this

economy.

- **Give No Benefits**
- Make a **"Who Cares"** statement such as "I am #1" or "Top Producer" or "We're The Biggest" or "We're The Best" or **"We Have 220 years of Combined Experience"**
- Run your ads without a Direct Response Message
- Use corny slogans or gimmicks

This is a major problem in the industry,

BUT it's a major <u>Opportunity</u> for YOU my friend…<u>ACT NOW!</u>

<u>Note:</u> Your **USP** must be unique so that it separates you from your competition and prospects want to do business with you. Why do you need to be different…

…Because if you are marketing like all your competitors, *a carbon copy*, then you should expect everybody else's results…which are meager and unsatisfactory. Use you **USP** to your advantage and profit from it.

NOT IDENTIFYING YOUR TARGET MARKET...
YOUR NICHE

Who Are You Going To Target With Your Marketing Efforts?

Many small business owners skip this part of their business planning or just out right neglect to tackle this critical step. Once you start this step, you may be overcome by fear and scarcity.

Why? You may ask! Because if you will narrow your product to specific prospects, which in turn you fear that you will **miss out** on sales to thousands of potential prospects.

This is the biggest misconception or mistake small business owners make by not narrowing their target market...their ideal customers, clients or patients.

Hear me out! You did not start your business to serve everyone on planet earth. Your business will serve a very specific group of people. Your herd. Your tribe. Your community. Your ideal clients, customers, or patients.

So who is your ideal customer, client, or patient?

<u>Whom will your business serve?</u>

You must at all costs identify the most ideal person for your product or service...this will be your perfect ideal customer, client, or patient.

The easiest and quickest way to attract your ideal clients is to identify them so that all of your marketing material will be written specifically for them. This will make it easier to engage and retain your clients for life!

You can't market to everyone because when you marketing to everyone, you're marketing to no one!

If you try to be all things to all your suspects (prospects), you will water down your marketing effectiveness.

It's very critical and important to know and understand who your message is for. You must select your target market so you can laser focus your marketing efforts and be very efficient with your marketing dollars.

Your marketing should be specific to your group *(target market)* of people...the people you will serve best.

Who will benefit the most from your product or services?

- *Who are you trying to convert from suspect to prospect?*
- *Who are you trying to attract into your business?*
- *Who are you trying to attract to your website?*
- *Who are you trying to convert to a faithful, loyal, raving customer?*

In order to answer all of those questions, you need to define who your ideal customer, client, or patient is.

Stop wasting your money, time, and energy on people who don't need your service or product. You need to be very specific in your marketing so you can attract your best customers or clients who are willing to pay for your service, regardless of price.

For example, if you are marketing to dentists, you need to be more specific: I am marketing to dentists in my area who've been in business for two years or more, who are between the ages of 35 to 45, have children, and specialize in children. This is your target market.

This is important so you are not wasting your marketing and advertising dollars on people who do not want your product or service.

The more you target to these people and the more they buy from you, the more you will understand their needs and wants. Your

marketing message will eventually match perfectly to them.
And, of course, you will attract other customers or clients who don't fit that specific criteria, and you will do business with them as well.

Everything that you create within your marketing material -- website, newspaper ads, radio, postcards, workshops--should speak to one person, but at the same time, you are marketing to many people. Here are your *7 Secrets to Attracting More Of Your Ideal Clients*.

<u>**Here are**</u> **The 7 Instantly-Effective Steps** to getting a stampede of new, paying customers, clients, or patients. *(You will never again have to worry about where your next client is coming from.)*

1. What is keeping your prospects awake at night…

What problem is keeping them up at night? What is bothering them? If your product or service can solve that problem for them, you will have a much greater chance of converting them into loyal clients for life.

The bigger the problem they have that you can solve, the more they will pay for that product or service.

When you started your business, what kept you up at night? Did you have zero-to-few customers or clients every week or month. Were you asking yourself, "How can I get more clients to stay in business, pay my bills, and feed my family? How am I going to make more money?"

How can I get prospects to call me who are interested in my services? That's what kept me up late at night.

What's keeping you up at night?

2. What do they secretly desire the most?

In other words, what is their main motivating for purchasing your product or service? For example, my clients' motivating factor for using my services is that they want to consistently attract all the customers they want or need every single month...no more wondering if they are going to make it this month.

But this is just the main surface reason they pay for my services. The deep underlying reason is that they can now live the life they always wanted as a successful small business owner and spend time with family and friends without worrying where their next customer, client, or patient will come from.

This is very, very powerful. This is an emotional, deep, driving factor. If you know what your ideal client's deep underlying motivating factor is, it can make you a lot of money in your business.

You can help your prospect get what they want and you get what you want too! Yeah! Amen!

All of this powerful information will be used in all your marketing materials to market specifically for them.

3. Who is selling something similar to your prospects?

Have your competitors tried to sell something to them and totally screwed up on their product or service? Are your prospects upset and angry because of this? What was the reason your competitor couldn't solve that prospect's problem? These are things you need to know so you can solve their problems much more effectively than your competitors can. My *Ultimate Client Attraction System in a Box* can help you do that.

4. What is your competitive advantage?

How are you different than all your competitors? Why should prospects do business with you? How are you different from everyone else?

What is the reason you are in the market in the first place?

5. How old is your prospect, is there age bias, gender bias?

If you've been in business for at least two years or more, then you can probably look at your database of clients and determine if there is an age or gender bias. You do have a database of your customers or clients…Right? I sure hope so because you're missing out on a **GOLD MINE**.

Who is purchasing your product or service? Are there more men than women who use your service or products?

This is very very important to know and understand so your marketing message can be very specific…marketing to men is different from marketing to women.

> *What appeals to each one and what is his or her underlying motivating factor?*

Again, you can make boatloads of money knowing this information…these are your ideal customers, clients, or patients who are ready and willing to do business with you because you can solve their problems…and they have the money.

This also helps you find a list of prospects that fit that exact criteria.

> *When you match your marketing to your specific ideal prospects, you can suck cash out of your prospects pocket's like a* **Hoover** *on steroids!*

6. Does your specific target market have children?

If your ideal prospects have children, your marketing message can be very laser focused and different messages can be created, so they can raise their hands and say,

> *"I am ready to purchase your product or service so you can solve my problem. Tell me what to do next."*

In your marketing message, make sure you give clear instructions about what you want your prospects to do, such as,

"Go to my website and fill out the form," or **"Call this number and ask for Martha, and she will get everything ready for you."**

There are many elements you can market to parents with children as they have different concerns than prospects who don't have children.

For example, based on research, adults without children base their buying decision 59% on quality, whereas adults with children base their buying decision 49% on quality. Knowing this information, you can create a premium package for your product or services and charge more when targeting adults without children who focus on quality.

When targeting adults with children, you can create a basic package of your product or service to entice parents who are concern about price. Again, your message will be different for each of these groups.

**Use This As Your Advantage To Gain
A Competitive Edge Over Your Competitors.**

Believe me, the majority of small business owners are not doing this type of marketing...they market to everyone which means they are marketing to <u>no one</u>.

You will be way ahead of the game!

7. What is their income level and where do they live?

Knowing how much money your prospects make tells you to some extent how much you can charge for your products or services. The more they make, the more you can charge or create a premium product to charge more. You can charge more but work with less customers, clients, or patients...And have more time off!

Marketing to a dentist is not the same as marketing to a beautician. Income levels are very different and the language they speak is different as well.

Again, you create a specific message-to-market match to have a much higher response rate from your marketing campaigns.

The question you should be asking yourself is, "Does my specific market make enough money to purchase my products or services." If they don't, then find another group, herd, tribe, community.

Where do these prospects live? Find out how far away from your business they live and are they willing to drive the distance to purchase your products. Are there incentives you can give for prospects that drive more than 30 miles to come to your store or business?

These are the **7 instantly-effective steps to getting a stampede of new, paying clients,** *so you will never again have to worry about where your next client is coming from.*

So, here's what you need to do so you can have the income you need every month to stay in business and live the life you want without chasing, bribing and fighting customers, clients, or patients on price. No **MORE** having customers or clients constantly nickel-ing and dime-ing you on price.

I go into much more detail in my **FREE** Module 1: Defining Your Ideal Customer…*Developing Your Niche Market*. This is part of your **FREE** bonus for purchasing this book. And don't forget to take advantage of my FREE **Roadmap Success Succession**. This is literally a $497 value.

Visit My Site To Get Your FREE Bonuses!

www.luminarmarketing.com/bookbonuses

NOT HAVING A LEAD GENERATION SYSTEM

Mistake 4

The key to any small business success comes down to **Three Things**:

1. Generating **NEW** leads every month

2. Converting suspects *(leads)* to **paying** customers, clients or patients

3. And getting repeat business and **referrals** from your raving fans.

Again, let me say that there are only three ways to grow your business. The number one way the majority of small business owners grow their business is by consistently getting new customers, clients, or patients.

You need a constant flow of new customers, clients or patients, but you also need to cultivate those new customers to increase your referral base business….*more about that later.*

You must have a systematic process for attracting new prospects every week or month and converting them to paying customers who stay with you and refer more customers to you…

…Assuming you are giving them outstanding customer service and your product or service is solving their immediate problems

There's no one single way to attract more prospects to your business as each business is different. But there is a system that any business can use to attract more of its ideal customers, clients, or patients.

Without a lead generation system, you will be reinventing the wheel every single time. This will cost you more marketing dollars every time and wasted time on people who do not want to do business with you.

Effective marketing systems will tremendously save you time and money, and help you achieve consistent and predictable results…Higher Return On Your Marketing Investment.

So, let's look at a three-step process that you can immediately implement in your business.

Your Three Step Lead Generation System

Step 1: Get prospect's attention and capture their contact information or have them come to you
Step 2: Convert those prospects into paying customers and give them **WOW** service
Step 3: Implement a referral system so they can constantly send you high quality prospects.

> **Get prospects' attention and capture their contact information or have them come to you!**

Here are some steps to get prospects' attention, make them raise their hands, give you their information, and convert them to high paying customers, clients, or patients for a long time.

First, you must get prospects' attention with your direct response message so they can raise their hands, identify themselves, and call you or go to your brick and mortar store. Identify the **PROBLEM** that needs to be solved…what problem are they facing that needs full attention **NOW!**

- Run your Direct Response Lead Generators to compel prospects to call you

    - Classified ads
    - Signs
    - Flyers
    - Post cards using direct response marketing
    - Post cards using *Send Out Cards System* that can run on Autopilot
    - www.luminarmarketing.com/sendoutcards.com

- Social media
- Website
- Blog

Second, you must get these prospects to sort themselves out into those who are ready-to-act versus those who are still wondering and working within a longer period. Again, this will depend on the business and industry that you are in.

Agitate the problem they are facing, **SHOW** them how you can solve their problem, and tell them to **TAKE ACTION.**

- Use an **800** call capture system to capture their information
- Use your **website** to capture their information
- Use your business **Facebook** page to capture their information
- Use Aweber, Mailchimp, or Constant Contact to Sift and Sort your best prospects…eliminate time wasters immediately.

Third, convince these high quality prospects to meet with you or go to your website so they can give you all their relevant information.

- Present your competitive advantage
- Present your compelling benefits
- Use your **USP**
- And convert prospects into long-term paying customers, clients or patients. So they can help you grow your business

Fourth, give them what they want with **WOW** service

- Give them more than what they ask if possible within your industry
- Do things differently than your competitors to stand out from the crowd. **WOW** them
- Reward them for being your customer, client, or patient

Finally, get referrals from them

- Communicate with these past customers, clients, or patients on a regular basis
- Monthly newsletter…this could be a simple one page newsletter
- Monthly newsletter postcard…a mini-newsletter
- Send the postcards on their birthday or holiday with the Send Out Cards System…set it and forget it on Autopilot.
www.luminarmarketing.com/sendoutcards

That's it. This is how you can attract high quality prospects that you can convert to high paying customers, clients or patients. Have them refer all the business you want or need. This works in any industry. Your message will be a little different for each industry. But this stuff really works!

NOTE: Your message must always do the following four things:

- Identify the **PROBLEM** they are facing
- **AGITATE** the problem they are facing so they can feel the urgency of solving the problem
- Show them how **YOU** can solve their problem with your product or service
- Tell them **EXACTLY** what you want them to do…
    - Call you
    - Go to your website
    - Facebook page
    - Blog
    - Visit your store

NOT HAVING A SYSTEMATIC REFERRAL GENERATING SYSTEM

So why do you need a systematic referral generating system? Because customer service Doesn't always equate to lots of referrals, and word-of-mouth advertising and referrals are Not the same.

I am going to show you my **Ultimate Referral System**. We won't go into all the details but you will get a good picture of how it works and how you can use it in your business, regardless of what industry you are in.

The Ultimate Referral System

Here are 7 unique benefits of the **Send Out Cards System**:

Note: You don't have to use the Send Out Cards System…but it will be more expensive if you purchase regular postcards from any store.

1. It's **extremely** simple to use and setup
2. It gets people to *fall in love* with you and your product or service
3. It can be put on **100% Autopilot**. This is the best part
4. It works for **ANY** business you can think of
5. You can completely *personalize* and customize it
6. It's inexpensive. Really inexpensive
7. And you can get started for **FREE**

I use the **Send Out Cards System** in my business. It's an internet based greeting card relationship marketing system. Now, you don't have to use the *Send Out Card System* to do this, but it will be much easier and very inexpensive than the traditional greeting cards you purchase at any store.

The *Send Out Cards* allows you to…

…send out completely customized greeting cards with your own photos, words, and in our own handwriting, and with your own personal signature.

The Ultimate Referral System

1. Get's people to fall in love with you
2. Motivates people to tell all their friends and family about you
3. It's a totally turnkey, done-for-you, pushbutton simple system
4. It's completely automated, set-it-and-forget-it system
5. It's warm, personal and customized for your business
6. It scales easily with no additional effort (1 or 1500)
7. It's very inexpensive to implement (about 1/3 the cost).

www.luminarmarketing.com/sendoutcards.com

The great thing about it is that you can set up fully automated "*Sequential*" marketing campaigns for just about any occasion. You can send a two-fold personalized greeting card, with a picture in it for only $1.46 postage-paid *(as of 2017)*. **WOW!** That's an incredible price.

The system also allows you to send gifts too.

Let's look at **6 Killer Referral Strategies** You Can Immediately Implement with the Send Out Cards System.

Strategy # 1: Recognize people for giving you referrals

Immediately send a greeting card with Send Out Cards and include a gift…it could be a $5 gift certificate for *Starbucks, Jamba Juice* or *Pete's Coffee*. All done directly from your computer, iphone, or smart phone.

Here's what you could say,

"Hey Phil, just a quick note to say thank you for the referral you sent our way. We really appreciate you trusting in us to take care of your friends and family. As our appreciation, we included a $10 Starbucks gift card. Enjoy the coffee on us. Thanks Phil!"

It can simply be a hand written note to the person who referred a customer, client or patient. Just acknowledging them gives them a sense of importance and appreciation.

Strategy #2: You Must Ping Your Network Once Every 25 Days

In my early thirties, I was a manufacturing engineer. In the electronic industry, we used a low-level computer language to ensure a system was connected to the network by sending a signal (bit) which we call ping. If the system was connected to the network, then the "ping" would return positive. We then knew it was connected to the network and the cable was good too.

In a sense, you are doing the same when you communicate with your network every 25 days…you are pinging them to stay connected and reminding them that you are still thinking of them.

In his book, *Never Eat Alone*, Keith Ferrazzi state that "If 80 percent of success is as Woody Allen once said, just showing up, then 80 percent of building and maintaining relationships is just staying in touch. I call it 'pinging.' It's a quick, casual greeting, and it can be done in any number of creative ways."

Here's an excellent example:

Joe Girard became the "**World's Greatest Salesman**" 12 years in a row by sending out over 16,000 handwritten greeting cards every month! That's Right…Every Month! Ouch! Stiff fingers.

The *Send Out Cards System* has thousands of unique greeting cards you can send to your past customers, clients, or patients on Autopilot...just set it and forget it. No more stamp envelop licking.

Strategy # 3: Give Referrals and Be a Positive Connector for Your Network

Not only should you orchestrate referrals from your past customers, clients, or patients, but also give referrals to your valued customers...your network.

So how can you be a positive connector for your network? Well, have special events for the top people or groups within your network. This could be a luncheon or special event at a nearby theme park, whatever is convenient for you. The purpose is to get your network together so they can give referrals to each other. You are just the bridge, the connector to bring them together.

They will love you for this.

Another way is use the Send Out Cards System to send a greeting card promoting a vendor or a past customer, client, or patient who owns a business.

Here's an example:

Suppose you have a customer who's a CPA that you also use in your business. You send out a greeting card with your picture and his/her picture too and promoting him/her to your network of people.

The message in the greeting card would be like this:
(Side 1)
"Here's A Very Important Person That I think You Should Meet!"

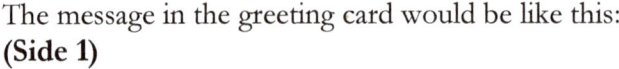

(Side 2)
"I'd like to introduce you to Ralph. Ralph is the best C.P.A in the Stockton area and will get your books in order, fast. If you are struggling to keep your books in order and wanting to find ways to

save money, then give Ralph a call at (209) 472-1411."

You also might want to add a picture of you and the person you are promoting.

You can do all this with the Send Our Cards System for as little as $1.46 including postage.

Strategy # 4: Start a Birthday Card Marketing System

With this system, **The 7 Biggest Fears Salespeople Face,** are no longer a **PROBLEM**:

1. No **Cold** Calling
2. No emailing
3. No **Networking**
4. No Advertising
5. No Publicity
6. No **Asking** for Referrals
7. No **Nagging, Chasing, Bribing** customers for referrals

So, let me lay this out for you and show you how this works. But to be successful, you must be consistent. Remember, marketing is not a one-shot thing; it must be systematic and consistent.

The Birthday Card Marketing System…

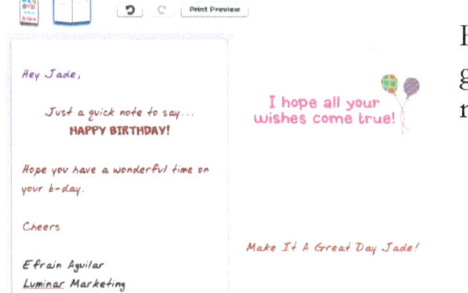

First, your monthly goal is to get at least 4 new clients every month from your referrals.

Goal: 4 New Customers, Clients or Patients Every Month From Your Referral Program.

Now, statistically speaking and conservatively, 10% to 15% of the people who Get Birthday Cards Will Refer at Least One Person that Month.

To get at least 4 new customers every month, you need to send at least 45 to 50 birthday cards every single month. This is all about numbers. So you must be consistent.

- **Approximately Per Day: 1.5 Birthday Cards Every Day**

- **Your Monthly Activity: 45-50 Birthday Cards Every month or…**

- **Your Yearly Activity: 540-600 Birthday Cards Every Year.**

So, 10% of 45 Birthday cards comes out to approximately 4.5 or 5 new customers, clients or patients every single month. Now this is going to vary depending on your business, product, or service.

But conservatively speaking, you are bound to get at least 3 to 4 new customers every month.

How much are 5 new customers worth to you? $5,000, $10,000 or more.

How much are 60 more new customers, clients or patients per year worth to you?

With the *Send Out Cards System*, you can fully **AUTOMATE** your birthday card marketing system! Set it and forget it.

You can also send small gifts to these people using the Send Out Cards System.

I will show you how in a short video later on. Hold on tight!

Strategy # 5: Have Lunch With a Prospective Referral Source twice a Month or More

So how do you do this and make it easy to meet with referral sources? You **AUTOMATE** Your Referral Lunch System!

First make a list of your top 50 to 100 most influential people with whom you want to establish or deepen your relationship and send them a "*Let's Do Lunch*" card once a month.
Here's what you can include in your greeting card:

"Meeting for lunch is an excellent opportunity to expand your circle of friends by getting to know smart, interesting people like you in a relaxing environment while enjoying a satisfying delicious meal."

Do this every month and you are guaranteed to get referrals from these relationships.

Strategy # 6: Ask Your Clients for Referrals on a Regular Basis…*Make It Exciting And Reward Them For The Referrals They Give You*

This strategy consist of a 6-month plan. What you do is send one greeting card to each new customer, client, or patient you get

- **Month 1**: Thank You Card
- **Month 2**: Referral Card (1)
- **Month 3**: Holiday Card…*(even if it's not a holiday, look for a strange holiday on that month)*
- **Month 4**: Referral Card (2)
- **Month 5**: Just Thinking of You Card
- **Month 6**: Referral Card (3)

You can completely **AUTOMATE** this with the *Send Out Cards System*…Very Simple, Easy, and Inexpensive To Use. There are pre-written cards specifically for referral campaigns.

You must try this unique **AWSOME** system that can revolutionize your business, life, and time. **Do It Now!**

**Check it out at:
www.luminarmarketing.com/sendoutcards**

NOT SEGMENTING YOUR LIST OF CUSTOMERS, CLIENTS, OR PATIENTS

The best way you can multiply your marketing dollars and increase the effectiveness of your marketing message is to segment your list.

When you segment your list, you can do the following with your marketing message

- You can test different messages for each group you segment
- You learn what works in each different group
- You can specifically speak to each different group for greater results.
- You can segment them by interest, needs, and wants

This increases the effectiveness of your Message-To-Market-Match, which means you laser focus your message to these specific segments based on their interests, needs, and wants. Mining the **GOLD** from your database.

This also doubles the chances of making a good sales or increase price to match each segment.

There are **Seven** unique ways to segment your list:

- *Buying frequency*
- *Purchase cycle*
- *Purchase amount*
- *Purchase types*
- *Pre-purchase*
- *Post-purchase*
- *Purchase by sex*

Again, this will depend on your type of business and the industry that you are in. You might just use two or three of the ways mentioned above. You have to determine what works for you best. But the key idea is to segment your list to increase the effectiveness of your message.

According to eMarketing.com and Target Marketing Magazine approximately 35% of email marketers that use segmentation see a better open rate. Direct Response Marketing, or direct mail users, also see an increase in their response rate.

Just a couple of tweaks here and there can dramatically increase your response rate, either online or through direct mail.

So Start Segmenting Your List Now!

In my coaching system, I teach you how to segment your list using a **Pricing Strategy Tool, P.S.T**. You can literally make thousands more per month on this single Pricing Strategy Too.

Ok, I know what you're thinking, *"My business is different"*, or *"I can't do that in my business."* I've heard this over and over with business owners who don't want to be creative or jump out of the box they've been ingrained in. You need to jump ship and start walking on water to stand out from the competition. Find a way to be different and apply it to your business.

NOT BEING A MASTER OF TIME MANAGEMENT

Not Enough Hours In A Day?

There a few things on planet earth that you can never bring back or gain back…one of them is **TIME**. Once time is gone, you can't bring it back or gain it back in any shape or form. So you must be a master of time management to laser focus on activities that make you money. Because once time disappears, it's gone for good.

The reason most business owners run around like chicken without their heads is because they don't manage their time wisely. But the real problem is **NOT** training your employees, vendors, customers, clients, or patients to work with you on your time and not theirs.

You must train them and clearly spell out when you can work with them. To help you out here, I will give you an example of how I use time management to train people to work with me.

Here is an example of my phone scripts to let people know when I will call them and work with them:

"Hi, this is "Efrain." I'm sorry I can't come to the phone right now. I'm either on the phone or currently helping a client. Please leave your name, phone number, and a detailed message so I can prepare myself in answering all of your questions. I return calls at three different times: at **10:30 am**, at **1:30 pm** *and then again at* **4:30pm**. *Thanks for calling and make it a great day!"*

That is the phone script I use every time, and my clients, vendors, and employees understand that my time is very valuable.

Your prospects, customers, clients, or patients will perceive you as being very professional. You'll be amazed at how people actually respect your time. Give it a try and see the difference it makes in your business.

Okay, I know what you are thinking. I will lose some of my prospects if I don't return their call immediately. Don't Worry! Prospects who want to do business with you will do all they can to get a hold of you. Those are the kind of prospects you want to work with…the kind that will jump thru hoops, climb over fences, and swim over rivers infested with sharks and crocodiles to get a hold of you so they can purchase your products or service and solve their problems.

Never be afraid to say **NO** to prospects who will…

> **…Suck Your Time And Energy Out of You Like A Hoover On Steroids!**

Manage your time wisely because once it is gone you can never get it back…with family, friends, and business. Guard your time like it's the last bottle of water on planet earth.

Now, here's a thought…If you are still lacking time every day, it's not because you are not a master of multi-tasking, but you are doing it way too much, and that's all you are doing all day long. This hinders your creativity. Period. Too much multi-tasking also lowers your IQ according to some scientists. So, **STOP** multi-tasking and focus on one thing at a time and the effects will be much more profitable in all areas of your business. Three things will happen:

1. Your productivity and accomplishments will increase on a weekly basis.
2. Your creativity will multiply and you will be able to solve problems with much more creativeness.
3. You will be able to manage your time-off with much more ease and enjoy life with family and friends.

FINAL THOUGHTS

Bonus Material

First, let's talk about the **Four C's** of *Small Business Entrepreneurs*. The Four C's are: *Control, Challenge, Creativity, and Cash.*

Control your schedule and business. When starting a small business, you must have control of your day-to-day activities or they will control you. You will be spinning in circles and have a very unproductive work schedule.

Challenges will come on a daily basis. You will have daily challenges that you must meet head on and solve; otherwise, they will escalate and cause more problems than they normally would. Don't be afraid to make bad decisions, as you won't have all the answers to your business problems. You will learn from your mistakes.

Creativity will separate you from your competitors. Be creative in all that you do, from creating new product or service to solving customers' problems. Set yourself apart by being creative in all areas of your business. Create new business process or business ideas that can generate income. Contribute to society by being creative with your business.

Cash is king. Keep track of your cash, especially your business expense cash that can disappear very quickly if you don't know where you are spending it. You must also remember that you need consistent cash to pay the bills to stay in business, even though the business is generating revenue. Your personal financial goals will also determine the amount of income you need to generate in your business. Your personal financial goals go hand-in-hand with your business financial goals. Set a goal to sell your business within seven to ten years, that is your exit plan. Not that you will sell it, but at least you will have a plan.

Always Be…S.M.A.R.T

Final word, don't be afraid to dream big in your business. Don't dream small, but set big dreams that are **S**imple, **M**easureable, **A**chievable, **R**easonable, and **T**imely completed. *Believe in yourself!*

Because sometimes no one else will believe in your dreams!

Conclusion

Thank you very much for reading my book, **The Ultimate Small Business Guide**...*Discover The 7 Biggest Makes Small Business Owners Make...And How To Avoid Them Like The Plague.* This book will help you avoid the most common mistakes most business owners make. You might have to shift into different gears to change the way you think about your business. But I guarantee it will help you grow in ways you didn't think possible.

One last word of advice, don't be a carbon copy of your counterparts. What do I mean? Do things differently from what your competition is doing, **ALWAYS.** Find ways to sell your product or service differently. You might be in an industry that has many restrictions and laws on how you market your service, but there are always ways to stand out...Be Different!

Make it a habit of doing things in a **UNIQUE** way to blow away your competition.

I have also included some resources you can use that will help your business.

Lastly, don't forget this **FIRST** step. Use this link to get a better picture of how the *Send Out Cards System* works and how you can start using it immediately and get started for **FREE**.

www.luminarmarketing.com/sendoutcards

WORLD'S GREATEST RESOURCES

United States Statistics
North American Industry Classification System.
www.census.gov/eos/www/naics

This is an industry classification code page.

Federal Citizen Information Center
www.publo.gsa.gov/smbuss.htm

The site has publications on small business, health care, copyright, trademark, and programs for the Americans with Disability Act.

The U.S. Census Bureau.
www.census.gov

The Economic Census
www.census.gov

The economic census will give you information on specific industries. You can find data on the number of businesses by industry in any zip code or county. Click on the economic census link.

County business patterns
www.census.gov/econ/cbp/index.html

This site contains annual reports on the number of business establishments by industry, size, payroll, and employees.

The Census Tract Street
http://censtats.census.gov

The locator provides information on county business patterns and international trade data.

American Factfinder
www.factfinder.census.gov
This is an easy to use site and features a very interactive menu to

search demographic information about the American people, city, zip code, and radius search.

Quickfacts
http://quickfacts.census.gov
This site offers demographic data at the national, state, and local level.

Current Industrial Reports
www.census.gov/manufacturing/cir/index.html

The site provides more than 100 current industrial reports that provide detailed data on thousands of manufactured products.

Fed-Stats
www.fedstats.gov
The site provides valuable information from over 100 government agencies and government statistical agencies.

Internal Revenue Service
www.irs.gov/taxstats

This site provides tax statistics based on income. However, this is a little more complex to navigate.

Edgar Database
www.sec.gov/edgar.shtml

This data provides financial reports from publicly traded companies. Enter the company name to search for a report.

State Data Centers
www.census.gov/sdc
This site provides statewide economic statistics.

The Ultimate Small Business Guide

Bonus Material

Here's a list of your <u>FREE</u> Marketing Bonus Materials:

1. Your 7-Step One Page Marketing Plan
2. Choosing **Your Ideal** Customers, Clients or Patients…*Niche*
3. Your Business **CPR-E**
4. **10 Marketing Tips** for Business **Growth & Profits**
5. Your 7.5 Gold Goal Setting Steps
6. **FREE** *Roadmap Success Session*..a $697 Value
7. Business Growth Multipliers…First Month **FREE**
8. Send Out Cards System…Send a **FREE** Card
9. *Cash Flow Surge* Marketing Tool Kit System…a $497 Value
10. Your WOW Factor Formula Report

To Get Your **FREE** Bonuses, Please Visit My Website To Download These **FREE** Bonus Materials. Your Password is **TUSMG7BM**

www.luminarmarketing.com/BookBonuses

Do It Right Now!

ABOUT THE AUTHOR

Efrain is a small business marketing specialist that helps small business owners like yourself attract more of your best customers, clients or patients..without having to chase, bribe, and nickel-ing and dime-ing you on price. Efrain understands the struggles you face as a small business owner when having to make income to support your family.

If you have children and own a small business, Efrain truly understand the struggles, fears, and anxiety you face every day to make ends meet to support your family. He now shares the secrets he has discovered by trial and error, and wants to help you **AVOID** those common mistakes small business owner make. Let Efrain Aguilar help you grow your business with these creative marketing strategies that you can easily implement in your business…regardless of the type of business you have!

Efrain Aguilar, MBA
6507 Pacific Ave
PMB 215
Stockton, CA 95207
www.luminarmarketing.com
www.luminarmarketing.com/bookbonuses
www.luminarmarketing.com/sendoutcards
Efrain@luminarmarketing.com

www.ingramcontent.com/pod-product-compliance
Lightning Source LLC
Chambersburg PA
CBHW041109180526
45172CB00001B/176